RIDDLES & RHYMES

FOR KIDS, PARENTS & EDUCATORS

FUN POPULAR THEMES

By Anita Vermeer, M.Ed.

Dedication:

This book is dedicated to all the passionate people that devote so much of themselves to supporting young children. A special thank you to those educators who work directly with the children. Your love and dedication to supporting the range of individual needs is remarkable.

RIDDLES & RHYMES

FUN POPULAR THEMES

WHY THIS BOOK

Young children are naturally curious and these rhyming riddles provide an engaging way to embed imagination and captivate their attention. Children become more interested when they know there is a missing word at the end of each riddle to solve.

As an educator or a parent you know that for most children, their learning will be reinforced when curiosity is connected to learning objectives. To support this, adults can be explicit about learning objectives when using this book with children. For example, just reading these riddles with children may or may not teach them that words rhyme, but explicitly labeling the words that rhyme may support that learning. Children may also develop metacognition skills through these explicit forms of modeling. Therefore, regardless of how you decide to use this book, I encourage you use language such as: "Oh, I noticed, those words rhyme, house and mouse."

POTENTIAL LEARNING OBJECTIVES:

- Children will recognize and identify words that rhyme

- Children will use a word to rhyme with another word given to them

- Children will use deductive reasoning skills to solve the riddles

- Children will use rhyming skills to solve the riddle

- Children will build conceptual knowledge on similar topics

- Children will build new vocabulary and descriptive language

INSTRUCTIONAL IDEAS:

Many of the ideas below are tailored for the classroom. However, parents can easily make some minor adjustments to using them at home. For example, a morning message can be posted on a kitchen refrigerator just as easily as it is can be posted on a chart paper in a classroom. Some ideas can be embedded into large or small group activities, or some may work better through individual settings. The needs of each child needs to be considered in order to maximize the learning potential.

1. Read a riddle with a child and ask them to guess what it might be based on the descriptive clues.

2. Read a riddle with a child and ask them to guess what else rhymes with the clue.

3. Give each child a picture and word of a riddle. Read the riddle and have the children listen to see if their picture and word matches the riddle.

4. Choose a riddle that aligns with a book or topic of study and write it on a chart paper or project it digitally. At circle time or in small groups, work together to solve it.

5. Similar to above, but give each child an answer card with a picture/word on it. Use these to let the children find who has the answer. Use the words at the back of this book to support this idea.

6. Digitally have the riddles on a projector with digital pictures/answers. Have the children find the correct match.

7. In small group or a learning center (with adult reading support as needed), have the riddles and answer cards separated on card stock. Let the children match them.

8. Make a copy of a riddle page and write the answers on a word bank sheet. Have the children use the word bank to write the answers on their sheet (Suggestion: Best used with children that are already reading.)

9. Review the Word Card activity section for more ideas.

10. Use the white space on each theme page to place post it notes as you monitor responses throughout the activity

11. For more ideas follow @AnitaVermeer27

Little paws that climb a tree,
Whiskers and big eyes on me.
I like to sleep on the door mat,
I have a long tail I'm a _____ .

ADDITIONAL IDEAS FOR PARENTS:
(Or Educators)

Play a rhyming game when on the move such as in the car, or on a walk. The game is simple by saying the word of an object you see or think of, and then taking turns saying as many words that rhymes as you can. It's okay if the words are not real words as the point is to practice the rhyming. For example, say you've seen a bus, then rhyming words could be gus, mus, hus, or wus. If your child says a word that doesn't rhyme repeat the words and add a rhyme word. Then tell them the two that rhyme and the one that doesn't and then play again.

Or, rather than focusing on rhyming, play what am I with your child by building on vocabulary using new adjectives and conceptual thinking. You can play this when you are on the go or when you are stuck waiting somewhere such as in a grocery store line or at a doctor's office. How the game works is tell your child "I'm thinking of a word that is (insert theme *such as a type of dessert)*". Then tell the child that you are going to give hints and they will have to guess. Then give the child a few clues along the way to help them guess. For example, "this type of dessert is round. This type of dessert is baked in the oven. This type of dessert is sliced into pieces to eat. What am I?"

THEMES:

The following are 15 popular themes used with young children throughout the year.

For more themes check out *"Fun Popular Themes TOO!"*

or for themes related to the seasons see book one

"Fun Seasonal Themes".

BEACH

Walk on top or play with me,
I'm everywhere for you to see.
Shovels and pails play this land,
Next to oceans you'll see _____ .

A rectangle shape and I lie flat,
Out on the sand is where I'm sat.
Time to dry off when you may howl,
Mom can you please pass my _____ .

Sitting on the sand is hot,
So bring me and have a spot.
Sit in me while you stare,
Because I am a beach _____ .

This is someone to watch you,
And beach safety's their job too.
Rules they follow really hard,
The person is a beach _____ .

With a shovel you use me,
Make a castle big to see.
With some sand and do not fail,
To have fun, play with your _____ .

Rub or spray this on your skin,
Protection from the sun's a win.
Or get sunburned is what is seen,
When you don't use _____ .

In the water at the beach,
You move your arms around to reach.
At the pool you're around the rim,
But at the beach you splash and _____ .

In the ocean waves are high,
And people ride them or they try.
In the water not on the turf,
On a board people will _____ .

BEDTIME

You read one of these at night,
On your bed but with a light.
At the pictures you will look,
While you read words in a _____ .

Lips will do this on your cheek,
Or on your forehead once a week.
Dreaming in your sleep is bliss,
After Mommy's good night _____ .

Go up these to bed at night,
And back down at morning light.
At the top is teddy bears,
'Cus your room is found _____ .

In your room is where I'll be,
Pillows and sheets cover me.
This is where you lay your head,
When you sleep it's in your _____ .

This bright light is in the sky,
night or day I don't know why.
When you see it bedtime's soon,
If it's night cus it's the _____ .

Two round things are on your face,
Above your nose is their place.
You may hear some lullabies,
When you sleep and close your _____ .

Imagination fun or wild,
When you're asleep or as a child.
Watch the sheep become a team,
When you drift off and start to _____ .

Bubbles, soap and cloth you use,
To wash your face and what you choose.
Do this before bed is prime,
To get all clean it is _____ .

COLORS

Leaves on flowers and leaves on trees,
A lime or pepper if you please.
You see me on a long bean,
Or the grass, 'cause I am _____ .

Bananas or flowers you may see me,
Or in the sunshine above the tree.
It's not the black on a bee fellow,
'Cause it is the color _____ .

This color is a metal type,
A ring or crown, but not a pipe.
End of the rainbow this is told,
You will find a pot of _____ .

A color you see in the sky,
Or in the water you know why.
Maybe you get something new,
When you buy jeans in _____ .

You see me on a clown nose,
Or on a berry or a rose.
On a stop sign it is said,
I'm not pink, but I am _____ .

Maybe orange is what you see,
And a fruit is what I'll be.
But add a brown tone like the beach,
And you'll know that I am _____ .

Lipstick, pigs, or a big bow,
Roses and flowers are for show.
Mix red and white I am the link,
Because I am the color _____ .

A horse, a bug, or on a dog,
I am the color on a log.
You see me all over town,
In the mud 'cause I am _____ .

CONSTRUCTION TOOLS

I hit things like pointy nails,
Joining things it never fails.
I make a noise like a whammer,
That's 'cause I am a _____ .

Many sizes I can be,
And I turn real easily.
Use me on a workbench,
Or on a car 'cause I'm a _____ .

Use a hammer to hit me,
I help you attach you see.
Often to wood I never fail,
When you choose to use a _____ .

In a hole I go round and round,
I tighten things is how I'm found.
Flat or Phillips are for you.
To use on me 'cause I'm a _____ .

I am a tool that's a rough type,
But on the wood is what I wipe.
Back and forth I am a shaper,
For smooth wood, I am sand _____ .

Use me on some wood or trees,
To cut the size that you please.
I'm super sharp more than a claw,
My blade can cut things I'm a _____ .

I'm a tool to sand the edge,
Of some door or wooden wedge.
Slimming things may take awhile,
But I'm a metal sanding _____ .

I have lots of little bits,
To help a screw in so it fits.
Make some holes as you will,
When you use me I'm a _____ .

ECONOMICS

I am a coin that is one cent,
Worth not much is what I meant.
In the car, you may find many,
But just one is called a _____ .

When you need something to do,
This is called the work for you.
No one can say that you're a snob,
When you work hard at your _____ .

Toys are not part of this group,
Clothes and shelter are in the loop.
Getting things that you can feed,
Yourself is something that's a _____ .

When you want something that you like,
A toy or fun thing like a bike.
Maybe a gift you want to flaunt,
It's not a need but it's a _____ .

Shop Inside to buy some things,
Like toys or clothes or fancy rings.
A sign may say open on the door,
When you shop inside a _____ .

This building is a place you use,
To cash checks and money news.
Saving money you will thank,
When you put it in the _____ .

Saving money takes some time,
But it will help you feel just fine.
Working harder you will learn,
As amounts of money you will _____ .

Safely keep your money here,
Your money's safe so do not fear.
When you want a big amount,
Save it in your bank _____ .

FAMILY

A boy or girl that may not talk,
Is real small and may not walk.
Climbs and crawls it is a maybe,
As it is a little _____ .

This is a sibling that's a girl,
Might do hair with a curl.
Your mom may say that she kissed her,
When she snuggles with your _____ .

A man that knows your mom or dad,
Throughout childhood and is glad.
He may like to eat some truckle,
And he can be a funny _____ .

He's a sibling that is a boy,
And you may like the same toy.
Share the same father or mother,
Because you call him your _____ .

This is someone that you like,
Helps you learn to ride a bike.
If you don't listen he might get mad,
But he loves you 'cause he's your _____ .

This lady loves you lots you know,
And she helps you as you grow.
A nursery rhyme is what she'll hum,
And cook or clean 'cause she's your _____ .

This is an older mom you know,
And to her house you often go.
She likes to visit at the spa,
To relax it is _____ .

This lady may not live with you,
But lots of love and giving too.
Always say can and never can't,
And be polite cus she's your _____ .

FARM ANIMALS

In the mud they roll around,
As they snort they have been found.
Most of them grow round and big,
One at a time is called a _____ .

These are mostly black or white,
They eat grass and do not bite.
Their soft wool we shave and keep,
'Cause they say baa they are some _____ .

A chicken type is what this is,
Top of the barn he will call his.
Hear this for a wake up booster,
Cock-A-Doodle-Doo says the _____ .

Brown and black are the usual kind,
Swimming at the pond you'll find.
I'm yellow in the tub for luck,
I say quack I am a _____ .

Brown or black spots on some white,
I eat the grass I see in sight.
Lucky milk comes out somehow,
For you to drink I am a _____ .

Usually you will see a pond,
Is where I live since I'm fond.
I like to sit on a wet log,
I might say ribbit I'm a _____ .

I have a mane and stand up tall,
Out in the grass or in a stall.
Trot or run I'm fast of course,
As I say neigh I am a _____ .

I help the farmer round the cows,
And I run next to the plows.
All the food I just might hog,
I woof and bark I am a _____ .

FOODS

A sandwich is what I make,
You can buy or freshly bake.
I'm happy when you are fed,
With some white or whole wheat _____ .

Purple, yellow or some blue,
A small and round fruit is for you.
It tastes real good in your tum,
I have a pit 'cause I'm a _____ .

I come directly from a cow,
I'm sure you know exactly how.
Non-dairy kind may be called silk,
But I am called the pure white _____ .

Hamburgers is what I make,
Or eat up a juicy steak.
This is something good to eat,
So you must know that I am _____ .

Lots of little round green things,
That's a veggie and not rings.
You need to ask and say please,
When you want to pass the _____ .

Long and skinny with green leaves,
It helps your eyes and not the bees.
A rabbit eats this not a parrot,
I am orange so I'm a _____ .

Oval shapes in white or brown,
At a farm or store in town.
From a chicken not their leg,
Fry or boil me I'm an _____ .

From an egg you must see,
I grow up and you eat me.
From a drumstick you are pickin',
To eat the delicious _____ .

HEALTH CARE

This is someone who is there,
To help the doctor and show care.
Some kind words is their verse,
When you say hi to the _____ .

This at home is where you sleep,
For a comfy place to keep.
I am where you rest your head,
You lie on me 'cause I'm a _____ .

When you're sick or when you're well,
You see me so I can tell.
For your exam I'm not a proctor,
I do the tests 'cause I'm a _____ .

Put me on, skin somewhere,
When it's cut, or has a tear.
To cover cuts is why I'm made,
So now you know I'm a _____ .

A hot temperature may seem,
When your body wants to scream.
Medicine can be a reliever,
When you're hot with a _____ .

This thing is used to see inside
That what is broken doesn't hide.
See my bones is what you'll say,
When you get an _____ .

To test how well your eyes can see,
Numbers and letters you read on me.
You try your very very best,
When you take an eye _____ .

For your throat or for your ears,
We shine this on to check you dears.
On your eyes it may seem bright,
When they shine the beam of _____ .

INSECTS

We are small and red or black,
And keep working without slack.
We like dirt not just your plants,
We are busy little _____ .

Black and yellow colors we are,
To pollinate the flowers far.
Try to get us if you please,
But we will sting you we are _____ .

I have some wings that you can see,
But I don't sting you like the bee.
I eat your food so I get by,
Inside houses 'cause I'm a _____ .

Red with black dots are on me,
They're my wings as you can see.
I know you wish that I could hug,
Because I'm a cute _____ .

Pretty colors are on my wings,
And on my head are antenna things.
My great big wings fly me up high,
Where you can see I'm a _____ .

After rain or dusk I'm out,
And will sting you without doubt.
When you move I will not go,
I like blood I'm a _____ .

I'm very ugly you will say,
And like the night rather than day.
I take charge just like a coach,
But I'm a bug that is a _____ .

I am loud you will hear me,
At night the noise is from my knee.
I can jump high to a fence picket,
Because I am a noisy _____ .

PETS

Little paws that climb a tree,
Whiskers and big eyes on me.
I like to sleep on the door mat,
I have a long tail I'm a _____ .

I can be a best friend to you,
I like to do some tricks for you.
I like to sniff to find a log,
I have fur 'cause I'm a _____ .

I sometimes have a fancy tail,
Or a big fin that helps me sail.
You keep me in a water dish,
Because I swim so I'm a _____ .

I have two wings so I can fly,
But a cage you often buy.
In the morning I can be heard,
As I chirp 'cause I'm a _____ .

Inside my cage I like to run,
Or a plastic ball is fun.
I am real tiny but I have fur,
I'm not a gerbil I'm a _____ .

Two long ears and a small tail,
At the pet store I'm on sale.
I chew carrots for a habit,
So you know I am a _____ .

One long body I do have,
And I hiss and do not laugh.
I shed my skin, which you may take,
I have no legs 'cause I'm a _____ .

I have legs and a long tail,
Change my colors I won't fail.
I can blend in like a wizard,
'Cause I am a type of _____ .

PLANTING

I like to make everything get wet,
From the rain or drink you get.
Want more of me when it gets hotter,
To drink or cool off with some _____ .

I'm on a plant but I have color,
Big petals or find some smaller.
I might grow tall up like a tower,
Tulips are a type of _____ .

As a seed grows you see me,
Eat from dirt and water's key.
I'm at the bottom like some boots,
As you know I must be _____ .

Pot of dirt or in the ground,
Lots of green leaves will be found.
Never stop and say you can't,
Take some time to grow a _____ .

This is up in the big sky,
Shining light and heat is why.
In the spring outdoors is fun,
Because plants grow out in the _____ .

In your grass or garden bed,
These tiny things can grow it's said.
Water and dirt are two needs,
And some sun to grow some _____ .

From the cloud I come down,
Make it wet all over town.
Water will go down the drain,
When there is a lot of _____ .

Under a tree you will find me,
I'm a cool place to sit you see.
The sun makes this a place for aid,
When you're hot and need the _____ .

PLAYGROUND

Swing across with arm strength,
All across the top bar length.
Feel like you can swing to mars,
When you go across monkey _____ .

On a climber I may be,
With a space under me.
Walk or run across this ridge,
I join two sides 'cause I'm a _____ .

On a climber you will find,
These are with a handrail kind.
You might climb up in some pairs,
Alternating feet up on the _____ .

I'm a big thing for you to use,
Climb or slide but wear your shoes.
Slow or fast there is no timer,
When you use the playground _____ .

This has small wheels under your feet,
You hold a bar but there's no seat.
An older kid may be a tutor,
To teach you how to ride a _____ .

Back and forth you go real fast,
When you're on it rocking past.
Long chains in place will hold these things,
As you sit and ride the _____ .

With my wheels and handle bar,
You may race me like a car.
With three wheels I'm called a trike,
You pedal me 'cause I'm a _____ .

I am a way to go down fast,
On your bottom it will last.
On your tummy you may have tried,
But feet first is on the _____ .

SCHOOL

Many colors you can use,
Like red, or yellow, or some blues.
Use a black to make it darker,
When you want to use a _____ .

This is used to write or draw,
Long and skinny like a straw.
Outline a drawing with a stencil,
Or start your own with a _____ .

This is an adult that you know,
To help you learn and help you grow.
They have a smile like a preacher
In your class it is your _____ .

Other kids that you must like,
To play some tag or take a hike.
Fun games you play that never ends,
When you're playing with your _____ .

Numbers and shapes you will study,
Or some graphing with a buddy.
You might count bubbles in your bath,
As you learn to do some _____ .

You do this when you take a look,
With your eyes and in a book.
Your eyes and fingers take the lead,
With the alphabet you will _____ .

White or purple in a stick,
Or pour it in a cup it's thick.
Used to attach a thing or two,
Some art or paper use some _____ .

Any color that you use,
To draw or scribble if you choose.
On the paper is the way on,
When you color with a _____ .

TRANSPORTATION

Lots of people ride on me,
Through a city for lots to see.
Little stops are made for us,
To pick up people to ride my _____ .

Different things are put in it,
And big wheels are made to fit.
I might take the trash you chuck,
When I am a garbage _____ .

Wheels I have a total of four,
You sit inside behind a door.
Travel near, or travel far,
When you ride inside a _____ .

Lots of clouds you will see,
When you sit inside of me.
Wind or snow or maybe rain,
I go up 'cause I'm an _____ .

I can be used for work or sport,
And different sizes of the sort.
I am something that can float,
So you must know that I'm a _____ .

Two black wheels and lots of metal,
Will go far if you can peddle.
Any color you may like,
If you want a brand new _____ .

Boxes are a part of me,
But big metal ones you see.
On the rail I have my own lane,
So now you know that I'm a _____ .

Straight up I go like to the moon,
One single stop and not back soon.
Count down from 10 before my trip,
I go to space I'm a _____ .

ANSWERS

BEACH

Sand
Towel
Chair
Lifeguards
Pail
Sunscreen
Swim
Surf

BEDTIME

Book
Kiss
Upstairs
Bed
Moon
Eyes
Dream
Bathtime

COLORS

Green
Yellow
Gold
Blue
Red
Peach
Pink
Brown

CONSTRUCTION TOOLS

Hammer
Wrench
Nail
Screw
Sandpaper
Saw
File
Drill

ECONOMICS

Penny
Job
Need
Want
Store
Bank
Earn
Account

FAMILY

Baby
Sister
Uncle
Brother
Dad
Mom
Grandma
Aunt

FARM ANIMALS

Pig
Sheep
Rooster
Duck
Cow
Frog
Horse
Dog

FOODS

Bread
Plum
Milk
Meat
Peas
Carrot
Egg
Chicken

HEALTH CARE

Nurse
Bed
Doctor
Bandaid
Fever
X-ray
Test
Light

INSECTS

Ants
Bees
Fly
Ladybug
Butterfly
Mosquito
Cockroach
Cricket

PETS

Cat
Dog
Fish
Bird
Hamster
Rabbit
Snake
Lizard

PLANTING

Water
Flower
Roots
Plant
Sun
Seeds
Rain
Shade

PLAYGROUND

Bars
Bridge
Stairs
Climber
Scooter
Swings
Bike
Slide

SCHOOL

Marker
Pencil
Teacher
Friends
Math
Read
Glue
Crayon

TRANSPORTATION

Bus
Truck
Car
Airplane
Boat
Bike
Train
Rocketship

WORD CARDS

These word cards are developed for you as a tool. They can support you with the rhyme riddles or you can use them in new ways to build vocabulary or literacy skills. Typically a child would need to have the decoding skills or sight word memory in order to be successful at using these word cards as they are printed. However, there are ways to simplify the use of these cards so they work well with younger children or beginner readers.

Activity Idea for Parents or Educators:

This activity saves you time in preparation work such as finding pictures, and will also help the child build some connection that each word has a meaning.

- Copy these words onto card stock and cut the word cards, separating the themes. If you are working with larger groups of children you might want to either make two copies of each theme, or plan to do two themes at time.

- Give each child a card and read them the word or if working with just one child you can give all 8 cards to one child.

- Have each child draw a picture of the word they received on the card on the front next to the printed word. For example, Child A may have a bike to draw, Child B some acorns, Child C some pie and so on. If you are working with just one child then you can have the child draw on all 8 cards.

- Unless time permits to do the next step on the same day, collect the cards or have the children put them in a safe space to do the next part on another day. (Note: Read the next step to decide if you want the child to put their name on the back or not before you collect them.)

- On another day, have the cards ready for a rhyme reading session. You may choose to put them in the center of a table and use them with an individual child or small group of children, or on a pocket chart with a larger group, or perhaps hand them back out to the class.

- As you read a rhyme have the children listen for the clue to word and encourage them to use the pictures to help them solve the riddle. If you handed the cards out to the individual child you can have them raise their card in the air when they hear their rhyme.

Challenging Activity Ideas:

- If you'd like to make this activity more challenging you can mix two or more sets of theme cards together and have the child identify the right card for the right rhyme.

- Or to support classification skills, you could encourage the child to sort the words into piles based on the topic such as sorting words that are Halloween, or words that are Christmas.

- For older children that are ready, you could encourage them to put the cards in alphabetical order or use them as flash cards to read or spell.

- Have the children draw the pictures on separate index cards and then play matching games to pair up the word with the picture.

sand	towel
chair	lifeguards
pail	sunscreen
swim	surf

BEDTIME WORDS

book	kiss
upstairs	bed
moon	eyes
dream	bathtime

green

yellow

gold

blue

red

peach

pink

brown

CONSTRUCTION TOOL WORDS

hammer	wrench
nail	screw
sandpaper	saw
file	drill

penny   job

need   want

store   bank

earn   account

baby	**sister**
uncle	**brother**
dad	**mom**
grandma	**aunt**

pig

sheep

rooster

duck

cow

frog

horse

dog

bread	plum
milk	meat
peas	carrot
egg	chicken

nurse

bed

doctor

bandaid

fever

x-ray

test

light

INSECT WORDS

ants	bees
fly	ladybug
butterfly	mosquito
cockroach	cricket

cat

dog

fish

bird

hamster

rabbit

snake

lizard

PLANTING WORDS

water	flower
roots	plant
sun	seeds
rain	shade

bars

bridge

stairs

climber

scooter

swings

bike

slide

SCHOOL WORDS

marker	pencil
teacher	friends
math	read
glue	crayon

TRANSPORTATION WORDS

bus

truck

car

airplane

boat

bike

train

rocketship

WHICH RHYMES?

These activities can be done independently or together with an adult. For independent work you can model how to complete the worksheet and then copy the pages for the children to do on their own. Or if you'd like to provide more adult support or prompts, you can copy the activity on a white board or chart paper and complete it together.

Beach Sample:

swim   howl

sand   rim

towel   turf

surf   land

Shovels and pails play this land,

Next to oceans you'll see sand.

Which Rhymes?

Draw a line to match the Beach word with a rhyming word.

swim	howl
sand	stare
towel	rim
surf	turf
chair	land

Complete the Beach rhymes.

Shovels and pails play this land,

Next to oceans you'll see _____.

Time to dry off when you howl,

Mom can you please pass my _____.

At the pool you're around the rim,

But at the beach you splash and _____.

Which Rhymes?

Draw a line to match the Bedtime word with a rhyming word.

moon	soon
bed	look
kiss	team
book	bliss
dream	head

Complete the Bedtime rhymes.

At the pictures you will look,

When you read words in a _____.

This is where you lay your head,

When you sleep it's in your _____.

Watch the sheep become a team,

When you drift off and start to _____.

Which Rhymes?

Draw a line to match the Colors word with a rhyming word.

pink	town
brown	link
gold	beach
red	told
peach	said

Complete the Colors rhymes.

End of the rainbow this is told,

You will find a pot of _____.

Mix red and white I am the link,

Because I am the color _____.

On a stop sign it is said,

I'm not pink, but I am _____.

Which Rhymes?

Draw a line to match the Construction Tool word with a rhyming word.

nail	shaper
hammer	will
paper	claw
drill	fail
saw	whammer

Complete the Construction Tool rhymes.

Often to wood I never fail,

When you choose to use a _____.

Back and forth I am a shaper,

For smooth wood, I am sand _____.

Make some holes as you will,

When you use me I'm a _____.

Which Rhymes?

Draw a line to match the Economics word with a rhyming word.

store	amount
earn	many
penny	door
account	thank
bank	learn

Complete the Economics rhymes.

A sign may say open on the door,

When you shop inside a _____.

In the car, you may find many,

But just one is called a _____.

Working harder you will learn,

As amounts of money you will _____.

Which Rhymes?

Draw a line to match the Family word with a rhyming word.

mom	mad
brother	truckle
uncle	hum
dad	maybe
baby	mother

Complete the Family rhymes.

Climbs and crawls it is a maybe

As it is a little _____.

A nursery rhyme is what she'll hum,

And cook or clean 'cause she's your _____.

Share the same father or mother,

Because you call him your _____.

Which Rhymes?

Draw a line to match the Farm Animal word with a rhyming word.

duck	log
pig	luck
frog	hog
dog	keep
sheep	big

Complete the Farm Animal rhymes.

Most of them grow round and big,

One at a time is called a _____.

I'm yellow in the tub for luck,

I say quack I am a _____.

I like to sit on a wet log,

I might say ribbit I'm a _____.

Which Rhymes?

Draw a line to match the Food word with a rhyming word.

meat	leg
milk	parrot
cheese	silk
egg	please
carrot	eat

Complete the Food rhymes.

A rabbit eats this not a parrot,

I am orange so I'm a _____.

From a chicken not their leg,

Fry or boil me I'm an _____.

Non-dairy kind may be called silk,

But I am called the pure white _____.

Which Rhymes?

Draw a line to match the Health Care word with a rhyming word.

nurse	say
doctor	verse
X-ray	proctor
test	head
bed	best

Complete the Health Care rhymes.

See my bones is what you'll say,

When you get an _____.

For your exam I'm not a proctor,

I do the tests 'cause I'm a _____.

I am where you rest your head,

You lie on me 'cause I'm a _____.

Which Rhymes?

Draw a line to match the Insect word with a rhyming word.

fly	please
ants	plants
roach	picket
bees	coach
cricket	why

Complete the Insect rhymes.

Try to get us if you please,

But we will sting you we are _____.

We like dirt not just your plants,

We are busy little _____.

I can jump high to a fence picket,

Because I am a noisy _____.

Which Rhymes?

Draw a line to match the Pet word with a rhyming word.

bird	log
rabbit	heard
dog	mat
fish	habit
cat	dish

Complete the Pet rhymes.

I like to sniff to find a log,

I have fur 'cause I'm a _____.

I chew carrots for a habit,

So you know I am a _____.

You keep me in a water dish,

Because I swim so I'm a _____.

Which Rhymes?

Draw a line to match the Planting word with a rhyming word.

seeds	drain
water	tower
flower	needs
rain	boots
roots	hotter

Complete the Planting rhymes.

Want more of me when it gets hotter,

To drink or cool off with some _____.

Water and dirt are two needs,

And some sun to grow some _____.

I might grow tall up like a tower,

Tulips are a type of _____.

Which Rhymes?

Draw a line to match the Playground word with a rhyming word.

climber	trike
rings	mars
bike	tutor
scooter	timer
bars	things

Complete the Playground rhymes.

Feel like you can swing to mars,

When you go across monkey _____.

Slow or fast there is no timer,

When you use the playground _____.

With three wheels I'm called a trike,

You pedal me 'cause I'm a _____.

Which Rhymes?

Draw a line to match the School word with a rhyming word.

math	lead
read	bath
friends	ends
glue	stencil
pencil	two

Complete the School rhymes.

Outline a drawing with a stencil,

Or start your own with a _____.

Fun games you play that never ends,

When you're playing with your _____.

Used to attach a thing or two,

Some art or paper use some _____.

Which Rhymes?

Draw a line to match the Transportation word with a rhyming word.

boat	lane
bike	far
truck	like
car	float
plane	chuck

Complete the Transportation rhymes.

I am something that can float,

So you must know that I'm a _____.

Any color you may like,

If you want a brand new _____.

I might take the trash you chuck,

When I am a garbage _____.

INSTRUCTIONAL CHART

This chart is available for you to use to monitor progress or to plan a theme.

www.ingramcontent.com/pod-product-compliance
Lightning Source LLC
Chambersburg PA
CBHW080630030426
42336CB00018B/3139